From Typewriters to Text Messages

How Communication Has Changed

Jennifer Boothroyd

Lerner Publications Company
Minneapolis

For my grandparents, who have happily shared their past with me

Copyright © 2012 by Lerner Publishing Group, Inc.

All rights reserved. International copyright secured. No part of this book may be reproduced, stored in a retrieval system, or transmitted in any form or by any means—electronic, mechanical, photocopying, recording, or otherwise—without the prior written permission of Lerner Publishing Group, Inc., except for the inclusion of brief quotations in an acknowledged review.

Lerner Publications Company
A division of Lerner Publishing Group, Inc.
241 First Avenue North
Minneapolis, MN 55401 U.S.A.

Website address: www.lernerbooks.com

Library of Congress Cataloging-in-Publication Data

Boothroyd, Jennifer, 1972–
    From typewriters to text messages: how communication has changed / by Jennifer Boothroyd.
        p.   cm. — (Lightning bolt books ™—Comparing past and present)
    Includes index.
    ISBN 978–0–7613–6745–1 (lib. bdg. : alk. paper)
    1. Communication—History—Juvenile literature. I. Title.
P91.2.B56 2012
302.2—dc22   2010045737

Manufactured in the United States of America
1 — CG — 7/15/11

Contents

Communication

Everybody communicates. Communicating is sharing thoughts and information.

You communicate when you talk to a friend.

People talk to one another. They draw pictures. They also might smile or nod their heads.

You can communicate without using words. Drawing is a way of communicating.

Some of the
ways we
communicate
have changed
over time.

Your grandparents
didn't grow up with cell
phones. They couldn't
use cell phones to
communicate.

Put it in Writing

People write messages to communicate.

Cards and letters are written communication.

In the past, people wrote messages by hand. Or they wrote on a typewriter.

Typewriters printed letters and numbers when people hit keys.

These days, people still write messages by hand. But many people send messages with computers too.

E-mail messages travel over the Internet. This boy uses a computer to send a message to his aunt.

Books and Newspapers

Writers communicate to readers in books and newspapers.

Newspapers tell people about things that have just happened.

The New York Times is a famous newspaper. Some people save newspapers from important dates in history.

In the past, people read newspapers twice a day.

Printers used to print two papers every day. They printed one in the morning and one in the evening.

These days, most newspapers arrive once a day. Many people read news over the Internet too.

New stories appear on the Internet all day long.

In the past, people printed
books on paper.

These days, people still print paper books. But people can read e-books too.

E-book means "electronic book."

Many people read
e-books on e-readers
like this one.

Radio and TV

Announcers and newscasters communicate over the radio and TV.

HEALTH CARE IN CUBA
▸ LOU DOBBS TONIGHT

LOU DOBBS .com

LIVE CNN

LISA SYLVESTER

UPDATE Plants shut for lead poisoning in south China; thousands sickened

TV communicates with sound and pictures. Radio just uses sound.

In the past, families gathered around the radio at home. They listened to radio shows.

Radio shows were like TV shows. But they told stories with only sound.

These days, people can play the radio almost anywhere. Radio stations broadcast music, sports, and talk shows.

People listen to the radio in their cars or on their computers.

The first TVs were small and boxy. The picture was in black and white.

These days, many people have large color TVs.

In the past, families got only a few TV channels.

Families in the 1950s picked from only a few shows at a time.

These days, people can get channels from around the world.

The Telephone

People talk with one another on the telephone. In the past, telephones were connected to wires. Sound traveled along the wires.

These days, some phones are still connected by wires. But we have cell phones too. Cell phones let people make calls from anywhere.

Cell phones aren't connected to wires.

25

Cell phones also let people type messages. Text messages are written messages sent from one cell phone to another.

New tools have changed the way people communicate. But they have not changed our need to communicate with one another.

Names to Know

These people helped to improve communication for people all over the world.

Tim Berners-Lee: In the 1990s, Tim Berners-Lee created the **World Wide Web.** This computer system made it easier to find information on the Internet.

Philo T. Farnsworth: In 1927, Philo T. Farnsworth created the first modern TV. Before his invention, televisions used motors and other moving parts. Philo's TV worked much better.

Reginald Fessenden: In 1906, Reginald Fessenden sent words and music by radio. This was the start of the radio we still hear in modern times.

Alexander Graham Bell: In 1876, Alexander Graham Bell invented the telephone. Only one person could talk on the first phone. The other person would listen.

Ray Tomlinson: In 1971, Ray Tomlinson invented e-mail. He wanted to send messages from his computer to other scientists.

Glossary

broadcast: to send sound or images by radio or television

cell phone: a portable phone that works by using signals sent over radio channels

communicate: to share thoughts and information

e-book: an electronic book. E-books can be read on devices called e-readers.

e-mail: an electronic message. E-mails are sent between computers.

Internet: a network of computers that connects people around the world

newscaster: someone who presents the news on TV or the radio

newspaper: a collection of news and information printed on large sheets of paper

radio: a device that sends or receives broadcasts through the air without wires

text message: a written message sent from one cell phone to another

typewriter: a machine that printed letters and numbers when people hit keys

Further Reading

FCC Kids Zone: History Page
http://www.fcc.gov/cgb/kidszone/history.html

Heinz, Brian. *Nathan of Yesteryear and Michael of Today.* Minneapolis: Millbrook Press, 2007.

Krull, Kathleen. *The Boy Who Invented TV: The Story of Philo Farnsworth.* New York: Alfred A. Knopf, 2009.

Oracle ThinkQuest: History of Communication
http://library.thinkquest.org/5729

Petrie, Kristin. *Telephones.* Edina, MN: ABDO Publishing, 2009.

Index

Photo Acknowledgments

The images in this book are used with the permission of: © Science and Society/SuperStock, pp. 2, 18, 24, 29 (top); © Asia Images/SuperStock, pp. 4, 5; © Blend Images/SuperStock, p. 6; © age fotostock/SuperStock, p. 7; © Fred Lyon/Time & Life Pictures/Getty Images, p. 8; © Flirt/SuperStock, p. 9; © Sam Bloomberg-Rissman/Blend Images/Alamy, p. 10; © Richard Levine/Alamy, p. 11; © SuperStock/SuperStock, pp. 12, 14; © FocusDigital/Alamy, p. 13; © F1 Online/SuperStock, pp. 15, 16; © Jeff Greenberg/Alamy, p. 17; © Cultura Limited/SuperStock, p. 19; © Science Photo Library/Photo Researchers, Inc., p. 20; © Flying Colours/Stone/Getty Images, p. 21; © IndexStock/SuperStock, p. 22; © Image Source/Getty Images, p. 23; © Scott Quinn Photography/Stockbyte/Getty Images, p. 25; © Katseyephoto/Dreamstime.com, p. 26; © Ariel Skelley/Blend Images/Getty Images, p. 27; AP Photo/Mike Groll, p. 28 (top); AP Photo, p. 28 (bottom); © Image Asset Management/SuperStock, p. 29 (middle); © Ed Quinn/CORBIS, p. 29 (bottom); © imagebroker.net/SuperStock, p. 30; © Joseph Barnell/SuperStock, p. 31.

Front cover: © George Marks/Retrofile RF/Getty Images (top); © Mike Kemp/Getty Images (bottom).

Main body text set in Johann Light 30/36.